TABLE OF CONTENTS

Introduction i

Photo Identification iii

Chapter 1   Gold Rush 1

Chapter 2   Construction 11

Chapter 3   Post Construction 37

Chapter 4   Other Operations 57

Chapter 5   Snow 65

Chapter 6   War Years 71

Chapter 7   Modern Day Operations 77

Chapter 8   Rolling Stock 89

            Railroad Facts 104

            Map 1 - Routes to the Gold Fields 3

            Map 2 - Chilkoot and White Pass Trails 10

            Map 3 - Summer and Winter Routes to Dawson 59

            Map 4 - White Pass and Yukon Route .... Back Cover

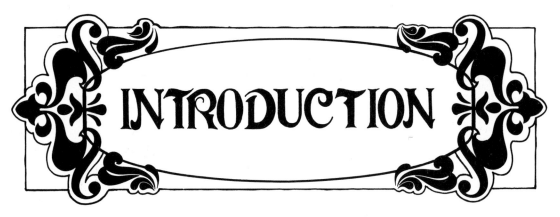

INTRODUCTION

If you are interested in railroad history --- particularly narrow-gauge history --- you should ride the White Pass Route from Skagway to Bennett or Whitehorse. If you are interested in the lore and legend of the Gold Rush years in the Yukon and Alaska, you should ride the White Pass Route. If you are interested in taking a thrilling train ride through some of the most spectacular scenery in North America, you should ride the White Pass Route. And if you are interested in a pleasant day of relaxation in scenic and historic surroundings, you should ride the White Pass Route.

I have ridden the White Pass Route (more formally, the White Pass and Yukon Route) three times. The first was in 1962, when I had a job in Alaska. Fourteen years later I rode the train again, this time with my wife, while I was doing research on the Klondike Gold Rush. We rode it again in 1979 while I was preparing material for this book.

After making the 110-mile journey from Skagway to Whitehorse in the comfort of a modern train, it is hard to imagine the hardships endured by the gold stampeders as they trekked across the mountain passes four score years ago. Yet the traveler lives with the reminders of the Gold Rush while riding this train, or while strolling the streets of Skagway or Whitehorse.

The Klondike Gold Rush spawned the railroad in 1898. The line was built to alleviate the hardships of the gruesome trip over the passes to the gold fields in the interior of the Yukon. By the time the railroad was completed in the summer of 1900 the rush was over, but the White Pass Route survived nevertheless, and has continued through the years to provide a vital link between the Yukon and the outside world. Today it is an integrated transportation system stretching from Vancouver, British Columbia, to Whitehorse, Yukon Territory, with subsidiaries reaching into the interior of the Yukon and other parts of northern Canada and Alaska.

I have tried to tell the history of the railroad mainly through photographs. The early photographers left a fantastic collection of pictures from the first days of construction. This book should be of interest to the thousands of people who ride the train every year as well as to railroad buffs who do not have the opportunity to come to the area. This is not the definitive history of the railroad, but I hope it provides an insight into the White Pass and Yukon's importance to the north country in the past 80 years.

Two things should be emphasized about the railroad. It is the last scheduled narrow-gauge freight railroad still operating in either the United States or Canada, and it is of paramount importance to the development of the Yukon. The newly opened Carcross-Skagway highway has taken some business from the railroad, but the White Pass Route remains the dominant transportation system in the area.

Many people have helped in the production of this book. A special thanks should go to James Hamilton, assistant manager for passenger sales and passenger representative for the railroad in Skagway, who offered tickets and advice. The staffs of the Yukon Archives, the Provincial Archives of British Columbia, the University of Washington Special Collections and the U. S. Army Archives were very helpful with the historical photographs. Barbara Kalen of Dedman's Photo Shop in Skagway provided much help with the new pictures. Bob McGiffert of Missoula, Montana, an exceptional, editor, put my sentences and punctuation into proper perspective.

I hope you will enjoy the history of this delightful and important railroad connecting the United States and Canada.

Stan Cohen

Author's Note: *The White Pass and Yukon Route has been closed since 1982 and the prospects of a start-up again grow dimmer as the years go by. Economic conditions in the Yukon, more precisely depressed metal prices, forced a shutdown of the Territory's mining concerns, the lifeblood of the railroad. Tourism has remained strong in Skagway and Whitehorse but tourism alone cannot keep a railroad operating the year around.*

Let us hope that conditions will improve enough in the future to allow this wonderful bit of history to again become operational.

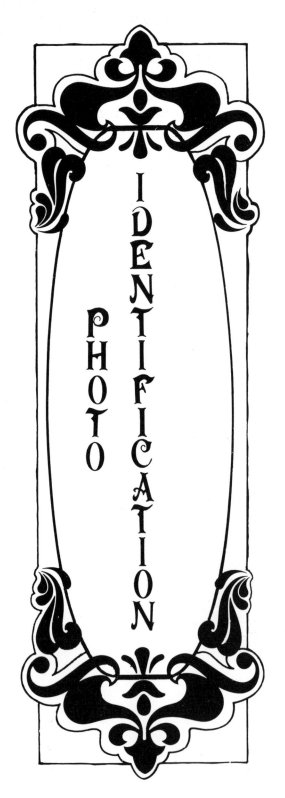

PHOTO IDENTIFICATION

Luckily, the White Pass Route has been well-photographed, especially during its construction period.

In the spring of 1898 Harrie C. Barley was hired as the company photographer. He spent two years documenting the construction and early operation of the railroad and left us with a remarkable record. E. A. Hegg, the most prolific photographer of the Gold Rush era, also left a large collection of pictures. The winter scenes are all the more remarkable because of difficulty of taking pictures on glass plates at the turn of the century.

Many other Gold Rush photographers left their record through the construction period, but good photographs taken in the years after that are in short supply.

I have tried to select pictures that cover the history and operation of the railroad from its inception until today's operation. The photographs were obtained from various sources in the United States and Canada. The sources and abbreviations used in credits are:

AA - Alaska Archives, Juneau
DP - Dedman's Photo Shop, Skagway
NPS - National Park Service
PABC - Provincial Archives of British Columbia, Victoria
SC - The author's personal collection
USA - United States Army Archives
UW - University of Washington Special Collections, Seattle
YA - Yukon Archives, Whitehorse

GOLD RUSH

"Gold," the magic word that has caused thousands of people through the ages to pull up their roots and go off to seek their fortunes, was flashed around the world in the summer of 1897 from the Klondike (or Klondyke). Many who headed there did not know the correct spelling, or for that matter just where it was that they were going. Most thought the gold fields were in Alaska, when actually they were in the Yukon in Canada.

This Gold Rush was to spawn a narrow-gauge railroad that would play an important part in the development of Alaska and northern Canada.

But before the railroad was even a thought in anyone's mind, thousands of stampeders had headed for the gold fields. The Klondike lay 650 miles north of the head of navigation at Skagway and Dyea, Alaska. In the summer and fall of 1897 stampeders by the thousands converged on these points.

The gold actually had been found in August 1896, by three prospectors on Indian Creek (now Bonanza Creek), a tributary of the Klondike River, but because of the remoteness of the area, word of the great find did not reach the outside world until a year later. When it did, it started one of the greatest mass exodus in North American history, with perhaps 100,000 people starting for the gold fields and up to 50,000 actually getting there.

Most of the richest gold-bearing streams, however, had already been staked by the thousands of prospectors -- many of them from the United States -- who had been in the Yukon area for years, and most of the later arrivals ended up working for wages, starting their own businesses or simply turning around and trudging out over the same route they had just taken in.

Although the gold fields were in Canada, 90 percent of the stampeders were from the United States and most of the gold was to go to American mints and into American pockets.

Dawson City, a former moose pasture a few miles from the gold fields, became the great metropolis of the North and at the height of the Gold Rush was the melting pot for more than 30,000 people. It was the largest city west of Winnipeg and north of Vancouver.

There were many ways to get to the gold fields, all of them expensive, difficult, or time-consuming. The easiest but slowest way was by ship from the West Coast to St. Michael, Alaska, and then up the Yukon River, a total distance of more than 4,000 miles. This voyage could take two to three months, and was a choice that

Newspapers around the world headlined the Gold Rush in July 1897.   UW

2

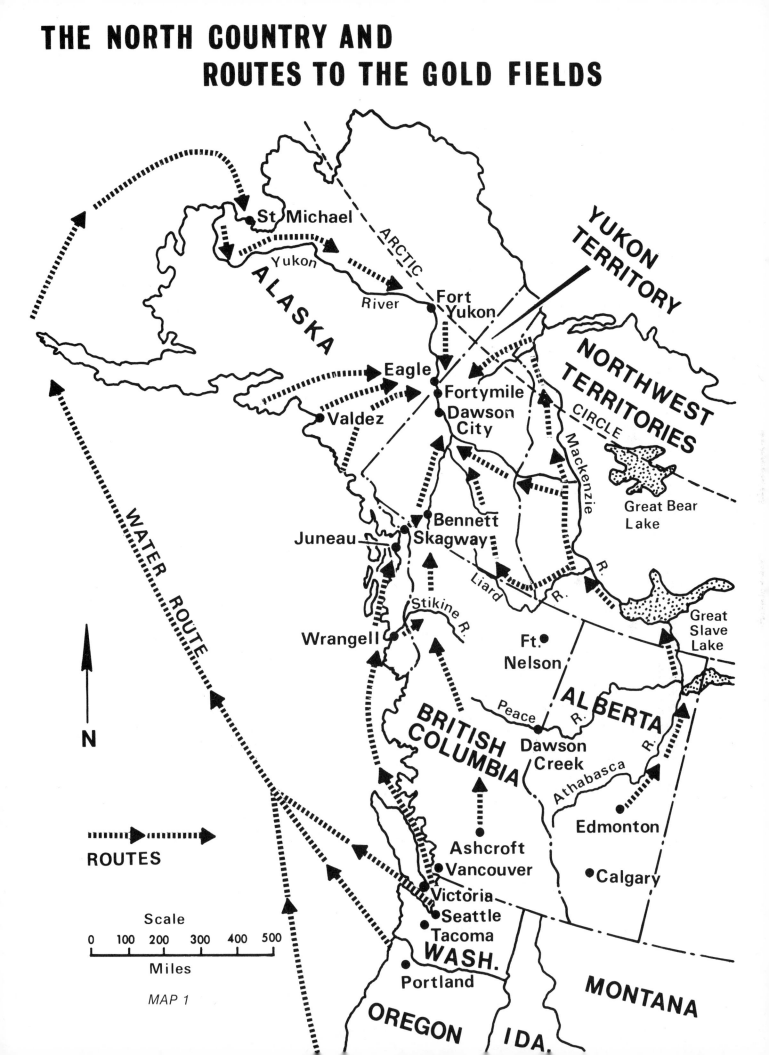

THE NORTH COUNTRY AND ROUTES TO THE GOLD FIELDS

St. Michael

ALASKA

Yukon

River

ARCTIC

Fort Yukon

YUKON TERRITORY

NORTHWEST TERRITORIES

Eagle

Fortymile
Dawson City

CIRCLE

Mackenzie

Great Bear Lake

Valdez

Juneau

Bennett
Skagway

R.

Great Slave Lake

WATER ROUTE

Stikine R.

Liard R.

Ft. Nelson

ALBERTA

Wrangell

N

Peace R.

BRITISH COLUMBIA

Dawson Creek

Athabasca R.

Edmonton

Calgary

→ → → ROUTES

Ashcroft
Vancouver

Scale

Victoria

0 100 200 300 400 500

Seattle
Tacoma

WASH.

Miles

Portland

MAP 1

MONTANA

OREGON   IDA.

was available only in summer. Other routes started from Ashcroft, British Columbia; Edmonton, Alberta, and Valdez, Alaska, but these traversed wild and nearly impassable country for hundreds of miles. Most men who started from these points never completed their journey.

The shortest and quickest way to get to the North was to take the Inside Passage route from the West Coast to Skagway or Dyea, Alaska; hike 30 to 40 miles by either the Chilkoot Trail or the White Pass Trail to Lake Bennett; build a boat and finally float 500 miles down the Yukon River to Dawson and the gold fields.

Most people preferred the Chilkoot Trail (from Dyea) to the White Pass Trail (from Skagway) as it was shorter and --- for the most part --- somewhat easier to walk over. At Chilkoot Pass the terrain was steeper than at White Pass, however, and the most memorable pictures of the Gold Rush show the stampeders trudging up Chilkoot's famous "golden stairs". The White Pass Trail was longer and although less steep it was very hard going for both men and animals. Unlike the Chilkoot, which was open most of the time year-round, the White Pass Trail was closed much of the time because of weather and poor trail conditions.

Gold Seekers on the beach at Skagway in 1897.   *PABC*

4

Broadway Street in Skagway in May 1898 was filled with prospectors, gamblers, confidence men, dance hall girls, businessmen and every kind of character from all over North America and many foreign countries. *DP*

Skagway in 1898. It had grown from a tent camp in 1897 to a city of more than 10,000 people in 1898. *UW*

Brackett's wagon road constructed part way up the White Pass Trail in the fall and winter of 1897-98. The right-of-way was purchased by the railroad at the start of construction. *YA*

Toll gate of Brackett's wagon road in 1898. *UW*

Looking down through cutoff canyon from one-half mile below the White Pass summit in March 1899. The White Pass Trail was not as steep as the Chilkoot Trail but because of the terrible trail conditions it was not used as much. It was, however, the better pass to build a railroad over. UW

People were backed up at Skagway for days at a time.

The famous Dead Horse Gulch, which can be viewed today from the railroad, got its name after gold-crazed stampedes drove thousands of horses into the gulch and then moved on up to the Pass, leaving the animals to die.

Whichever route a stampeder took, he wound up at Lake Bennett, more than 30 miles from tidewater. There he would build a boat --- and if he arrived in late fall, he would have to stay through the winter, waiting for the lake and river ice to break up in the spring.

By the time the railroad reached Lake Bennett on July 6, 1899, the zenith of the Klondike Gold Rush was past. There had been new discoveries -- at Atlin, British Columbia, in 1898, and at Nome, Alaska, earlier in 1899. The railroad created by the Gold Rush was completed too late to be a part of it. But it lived on to contribute enormously to the development of the Yukon.

Hauling 1400 pounds with one horse over the White Pass summit.　　　*UW*

The Canadian customs station at Log Cabin, British Columbia, in 1899. The prospectors had to check in here before proceeding to Lake Bennett.   *UW*

Lake Bennett in 1898. This was the largest tent city in the world, with more than 10,000 people waiting for the ice breakup in the spring of 1898 to start their trip to Dawson.   *YA*

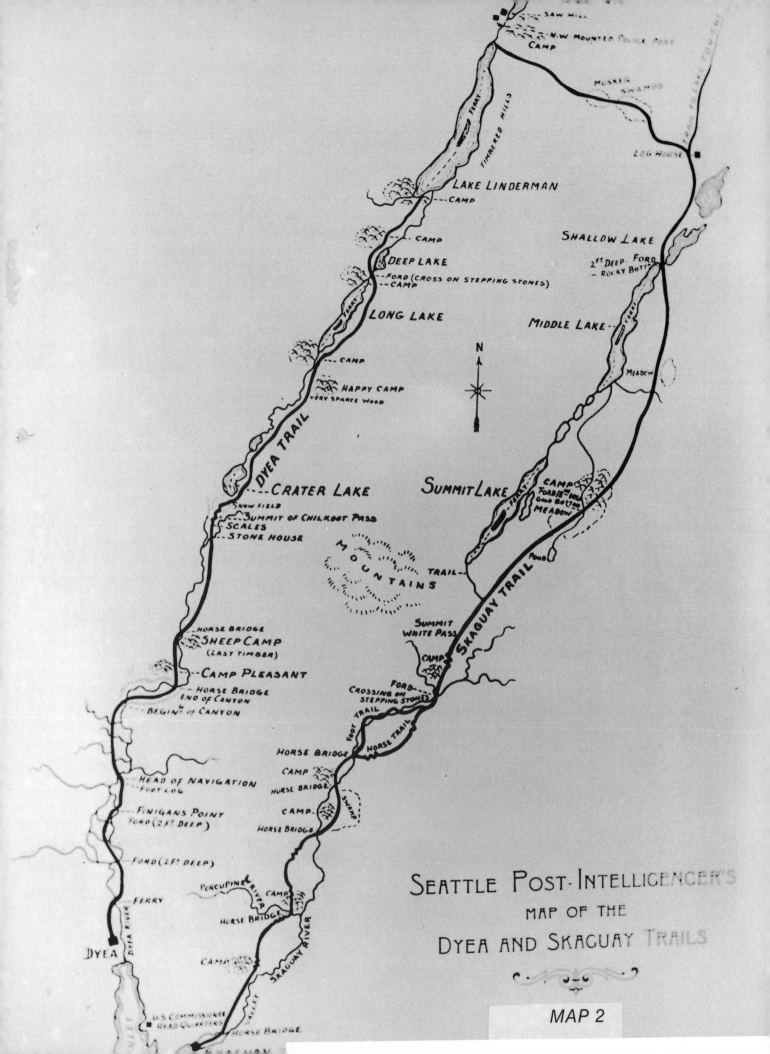

SAW MILL

N.W MOUNTED POLICE POST
CAMP

MUSKEG
SWAMPS

TRAIL THROUGH TIMBER

FERRY

TIMBERED HILLS

LOG HOUSE

LAKE LINDERMAN
--- CAMP

SHALLOW LAKE

--- CAMP

DEEP LAKE
--- FORD (CROSS ON STEPPING STONES)
--- CAMP

2ᶠᵗ DEEP FORD
-- ROCKY BOTTOM

LONG LAKE

FERRY

MIDDLE LAKE

--- CAMP

MEADOW

--- HAPPY CAMP
VERY SPARSE WOOD

N

SUMMIT LAKE

DYEA TRAIL

CRATER LAKE

SNOW FIELD
-- SUMMIT OF CHILKOOT PASS
SCALES
-- STONE HOUSE

CAMP
FORD
GOOD BOTTOM
MEADOW

FERRY

MOUNTAINS

TRAIL ---

SKAGUAY TRAIL

POND

-- HORSE BRIDGE
SHEEP CAMP
(LAST TIMBER)

SUMMIT
WHITE PASS

CAMP

-- CAMP PLEASANT
-- HORSE BRIDGE
END OF CANYON

FORD
CROSSING ON
STEPPING STONES

BEGIN OF CANYON

FOOT TRAIL

HORSE TRAIL

HORSE BRIDGE

HORSE TRAIL

CAMP

HORSE BRIDGE

-- HEAD OF NAVIGATION
FOOT LOG

CAMP

SWAMP

-- FINIGANS POINT
FORD (2 FT DEEP)

HORSE BRIDGE

FORD (2 FT DEEP)

PORCUPINE RIVER

CAMP

SEATTLE POST-INTELLIGENCER'S
MAP OF THE
DYEA AND SKAGUAY TRAILS

HORSE BRIDGE

FERRY

DYEA RIVER

DYEA

CAMP

SKAGUAY RIVER

U.S. COMMISSIONERS
HEAD QUARTERS

HORSE BRIDGE

SKAGUAY

MAP 2

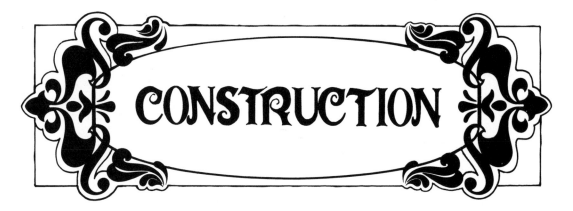

CONSTRUCTION

The need for a more efficient method of crossing the passes of the St. Elias Range from tidewater in Alaska to Lake Bennett in British Columbia became evident at the height of the Gold Rush in 1897.

The White Pass Trail had become increasingly difficult to traverse, and both it and the Chilkoot Trail further west were clogged with stampeders trying to get to the Klondike gold fields as quickly as possible.

Many improvements were undertaken on both trails in 1897 and 1898. Several aerial tramways were built over the Chilkoot, and a number of attempts were made to improve the White Pass.

George Brackett, an ex-mayor of Minneapolis and a former engineer on the Northern Pacific Railroad, was one of the first to try to improve the White Pass Trail. He helped organize the Skagway and Yukon Transportation and Improvement Company to build a wagon road. Capital stock was established at $300,000 and work on the wagon road began in November 1897, under Brackett's direction.

From the start, construction was hampered by insufficient funds and lack of an adequate survey of the proposed route. The incorporators failed to raise the needed capital and Brackett was able to complete only eight miles of his road before he ran out of money in December, 1897. He had to leave for the outside to raise more.

When he returned in June 1898, he had more money and he started charging tolls for use of the road. Fees for the eight miles were $10 for a wagon, $1 for a foot traveler and $1 for each animal. The stampeders refused to pay, and Brackett, using his influence in Washington, had the U. S. Army send troops from Dyea to maintain order and keep the road open.

With the east fork of the Skagway River bridged, the eight-mile road provided an easier way for the thousands of people to use the White Pass Trail. Still, something better was needed.

The idea for the railroad was born in the early part of 1898 at a meeting of two men who would eventually push the rails over the pass. One of them, Sir Thomas Tancrede, was a representative of a group of British financiers (Close Brothers). The other, Michael J. Heney, was a former Canadian railroad contractor who had helped build the Canadian Pacific.

Both men had come north with the idea of building a railroad over the mountains to get the men and materials to the gold fields.

Tancrede, who had come north with Samuel H. Graves of Chicago and E. C. Hawkins of Seattle, surveyed the mountains and concluded that because of the rugged terrain, a railroad was not feasible. Henry (who was known as "Big Mike" or "The Irish Prince") thought differently. He had viewed the mountains and had no qualms about building a railroad there.

After a night of talking in Skagway's St. James Hotel bar, he got Tancrede to agree to begin the project with financing from British backers. It would be an expensive undertaking that would require tons of equipment, thousands of men and reasonably good weather. All three items were lacking from the start.

The White Pass and Yukon Railroad Company was organized in April 1898.

The portion through Alaska was incorporated in the state of West Virginia as the Pacific and Arctic Railway and Navigation Company. The British backers also obtained charters for the right-of-way in British Columbia and the Yukon. The railroad in British Columbia was formed as the British Columbia Yukon Railway Company and in the Yukon as the British Yukon Railway Company. Samuel Graves was named president of the railroad and construction began in April 1898.

Brackett, who was still having trouble raising funds and was facing mounting difficulties with the American and Canadian governments, sold his right-of-way to the railroad for $50,000. He had invested $185,000 of his own money in the project.

The railroad men realized from the start that a standard-gauge (4'8½")

Working on the roadbed down Broadway in Skagway in June 1898.   UW

The temporary headquarters of the Pacific and Arctic Railway and Navigation Company (the White Pass Company in Alaska) in Skagway in 1898.   *YA*

Laying the rails at the north end of Skagway in September 1898. Tents and cabins of the city are in the background.   *YA*

Members of F. B. Flood's engineering corps pose with surveying instruments in front of their tent in September 1898.   *YA*

railway across the mountains would be too costly, so they settled on a three-foot narrow-gauge.

Since no accurate maps were available, several parties were sent out to survey possible routes to Lake Bennett, 40 miles from Skagway. Five surveys were brought back. The route chosen was the one over the original White Pass, discovered years before by Captain William Moore, the founder of Skagway.

Construction problems were encountered immediately. The railroad had to compete for ship cargo space with stampeders coming north from the West Coast. Thousands of workers were needed, but the stampeders had neither time nor inclination to work for wages with all that gold just waiting to be found in the Klondike.

A dispute arose over the location of the international border. The Canadians thought the border was at tidewater at Skagway; the Americans thought it was at Log Cabin, just beyond the White Pass summit. When the White Pass was finally agreed upon, considerable diplomacy was required to get Canada to permit the railroad to cross the border. And there was interference from a gang of outlaws operating out of Skagway under the direction of Jefferson Randolph Smith, better known as "Soapy Smith." The gang robbed new arrivals at Skagway, usually by confidence tricks, and caused trouble at the railroad work camps. But the problem disappeared abruptly on July 9, 1898. Soapy's gang had robbed a prospector of his gold two days before, and the anger of Skagway's citizens reached the flash point. Vigilantes organized, and one of them, Frank Reid, shot it out with Soapy on the Skagway waterfront wharf. Both men were killed. After Soapy's demise, his gang dispersed and the railroad crews and citizens of Skagway were no longer bothered by outlaws.

Enough material had arrived in April 1898, for rail lines to be laid down on Broadway Street, Skagway, to start the 40-mile route to Lake Bennett.

Henry was the chief of construction and had as assistants John Hislop, the chief surveyor, and E. C. Hawkins,, the chief engineer. An engineer named Brydon Jack was hired by the British backers to watch over their interests. Jack soon died of pneumonia, however, and the Britons put Hawkins on their Payroll to replace him.

Since the major base of supply for heavy equipment was Seattle and Vancouver, 1,000 miles away, the construction crews had to tackle the job of building a roadbed with the available picks and shovels until more sophisticated equipment could be shipped north. The construction crews were composed of men from around the world and from many different environments. Many highly educated people, some of them professional men, swung picks and wielded shovels for a few dollars a day. All had come north to mine the gold in the Klondike, but for one reason or another, were stuck in Skagway, and worked for the railroad to earn enough money to get to the gold fields or to return home. The number of men varied day by day from 2,000 to 700. A major gold strike or even a rumor of one was

Hand labor at the end of the grade near the summit on August 25, 1898.   YA

15

Railway workers used ropes to support themselves as they cut the railway grade on a steep face of Tunnel Mountain in September 1898. *YA*

Construction workers use sledge hammers to pound a steel rod into rock to make a hole for a blasting charge. *YA*

A portable blacksmith shop was a necessity for the railroad construction. This one at White Pass City in August 1898 is making horseshoes. The shop was essential for making and repairing tools and for keeping the horses shod. *YA*

A wooden hoist lifts heavy boulders. Many improvised methods were used to lighten the work. *YA*

Removing the rubble after blasting was back-breaking work. Thousands of men toiled with pick and shovel to cut the roadbed from solid rock.   *YA*

enough to deplete the ranks. Construction did proceed, however, and the summit of White Pass was reached on February 20, 1899. Rails had been scheduled to be at the summit by Christmas, 1898, but were delayed by poor weather and lack of manpower. The roadbed had to be blasted out of solid rock, and a 250-foot tunnel was blasted and dug out by hand through a solid granite mountainside. This was the only tunnel on the 110-mile route. In the 21 miles to the summit, the road-bed climbed from sea level at Skagway to 2,885 feet. The railroad seemed to hang on the mountainside for most of the way to the summit. Several wooden trestles were built along the mountainside, one of the longest crossing Glacier George.

A spectacular steel cantilever bridge was built across Dead Horse Gulch below the summit. It arched 215 feet above the gulch and at one time was the highest railroad bridge in the world. It took until 1901 to complete this engineering feat. A switch-back was used to get around the gulch until the bridge was completed.

Once the summit was crossed, construction became easier and the shore of Lake Bennett was reached on July 6, 1899.

Winter construction was very difficult in this country. The solid granite, rubbed smooth by ancient glaciers, provided no footholds for the workers. The winter wind was strong and the men had to be roped together. Temperatures fell from 30 degrees to 60 degrees below zero. By October 1898, the road-bed reached above timberline and the

Working on the grade at midnight in August 1898. The long summer nights provided many hours for construction.   *YA*

HENEY SATION
WHITE PASS AND YUKON ROUTE.

Heney Station below the summit.   *UW*

Building the only tunnel on the railroad. Hand labor and tools did the work after blasting was completed.   UW

weather got worse. Deep snow drifts produced hazardous working conditions.

Since the railroad was being cut into solid rock to the summit, no gravel for the roadbed was available along the way. It had to be hauled either from the bed of the Skagway River or from Fraser, beyond the summit.

But the construction men were well cared for. There were few serious accidents, little sickness, and plenty of food. Henry did not allow liquor at the camps and this had a lot to do with the work attitude of the men. The pay ranged up to $3.00 for a 10-hour day. Lodging ws free but meals had to be paid for.

The first train ran the 40 miles from Skagway to Lake Bennett on July 6, 1899. The next 27 miles lay along the lake, and crews were sent by water to establish work camps at intervals along the shore. Other crews started working south from Whitehorse in the summer of 1899. The Lake Bennett portion was hard to build because rock work was extensive and the underlying permafrost caused great problems with roadbed construction.

Freight could now be sent by train to Lake Bennett, put on lake steamers to Caribou Crossing (now Carcross) 27 miles away on the north end of the lake and then hauled to Whitehorse on wagons or by rail as the roadbed construction progressed. The railroad connected Carcross and Whitehorse in June 1900 and the entire line was completed on July 29, 1900, with a golden spike celebration at Carcross, Yukon Territory.

Many Canadian and American dignitaries were in attendance that day. A real golden spike was placed on a rail and many attempts were made to drive it in. But to no avail. The spike ended up a twisted piece of gold.

It had taken 27 months to build a 110-mile rail line. A long time for a short distance, perhaps, but considering the terrain, weather, manpower and machinery problems that the builders had to contend with, it is a tribute to their persistence and dedication that the railroad was completed at all.

Construction of the railroad in the winter of 1898-99.   *UW*

A track-mounted steam shovel and crew removing boulders from a landslide on the tracks.   *YA*

Working on the wooden trestle at the tunnel entrance in 1899.   *UW*

Workers at a construction camp wait for their pay after hearing of the Atlin gold strike in August 1898. YA

View of tents among the trees at Camp 8 near Glacier on November 20, 1898. Stove smoke is coming from the tents. YA

A tent kitchen at Camp 10 in July 1898. Tent camps were set up at various sites along the construction right-of way. YA

Mealtime in a mess tent. Providing good food and lots of it was a necessity to keep the workers fit and on the payroll, especially in winter. YA

The railroad yards in Skagway before the roundhouse was built in 1900.   YA

Railroad shops at Skagway after the roundhouse was built.   PABC

The summit camp on February 2, 1899.   UW

Summit of White Pass in March 1899.   PABC

The United States-Canada border and Summit Lake in 1899.   *UW*

The northbound and southbound trains meet at the summit station on April 9, 1899.   *UW*

28

The first passenger train on the White Pass summit, February 20, 1899.   *UW*

The early freight and passenger station at Log Cabin during the construction period. The wagons were used to haul the construction material. Log Cabin became a small town during the Gold Rush but was abandoned after the rush was over.   *UW*

Bennett in 1900, no longer the great tent city of 1898, but now an important stop on
the railroad.   *UW*

Driving the last spike at Lake Bennett on July 6, 1899. The mountain barrier had at
last been spanned by steel rails.   *UW*

The first passenger train leaves Bennett on July 6, 1899, carrying $500,000 in gold dust. *UW*

Freight at Bennett in September 1899. Before the railroad was completed to Carcross, freight had to be unloaded at Bennett and then loaded on steamers for the water journey to Carcross. *UW*

The bottom of a 48,000-cubic-yard cut for the railway that was excavated with scrapers between December 5, 1899, and January 6, 1900, when temperatures ranged from minus 30 degrees to minus 56 degrees. *YA*

Building the roadway across one of the numerous lakes north of the summit. Gravel had to be hauled from a pit at Fraser. *UW*

Carcross at the northern end of Lake Bennett in June 1900. Mainly a tent town, but an important railroad stop, it originally was named Caribou Crossing for the amount of caribou crossing the area. *YA*

Laying rails north of the summit near Camp 6. *UW*

Driving the last spike at Caribou (Carcross) on July 29, 1900. A great engineering feat had been accomplished.

YA

Driving the last spike at Whitehorse on June 8, 1900, two years after construction had begun. *YA*

View of Whitehorse in 1900. The railroad station in the center was still under construction. *YA*

POST CONSTRUCTION

After the railroad reached White-horse in the summer of 1900, regularly scheduled freight and passenger service was established to connect tidewater at Skagway with the riverboat service at Whitehorse. Finally there was a route to the Klondike gold fields.

But by 1900 the Klondike Gold Rush was over. Prospectors abandoned the Klondike creeks in droves to head for the new strike on the beaches of Nome, Alaska. The Klondike claims could no longer be worked profitably by hand, and were being consolidated by large concerns, to be worked either hydraulically or by dredging. Tremendous amounts of machinery and material, but relatively few men, were needed for the large operations.

The railroad had a good year in 1900. Then, despite demand for the hauling of the heavy equipment, business slacked off. Nevertheless, the large-scale gold operations in the Klondike area, plus discoveries of a large copper deposit near Whitehorse and lead, zinc and silver deposits at Mayo in the early part of the century kept the railroad operating with ore brought by river steamer to White-horse, where it was loaded on freight cars for Skagway.

This business, combined with the general freight and passenger service, barely kept the company solvent, however.

A 12-mile spur to the Whithorse copper mine was constructed in 1910 and this brought in additional freight revenue.

Up to World War I the railroad carried 10,000 to 15,000 passengers and up to 30,000 tons of freight a year. However, the line had to be reorganized financially in 1918 to keep from closing, for the roadbed and rolling stock were rapidly deteriorating as there was no money to upgrade them. No new locomotives were purchased between 1908 and 1938.

Ore shipments and tourists barely kept the railroad in business through the 1920s, but with the depression, the tourist business dried up, and freight shipments during the 30s averaged only about 12,000 tons a year.

Probably only the war kept the White Pass Route from becoming just another name in the histories of the Gold Rush era.

The development of natural resources in the Yukon kept business at a good level after the war. A typical year such as 1949 found the railroad operating, along with its rolling stock, six river steamers, two motor ships, 11 barges and the passenger steamer Tulshi operating on Tagish Lake east of Lake Bennett. Four thousand passengers were carried on the railroad and 1700 on the river steamers.

Skagway in 1900. The Gold Rush boom was over and the town had settled down as a railroad and trading center. UW

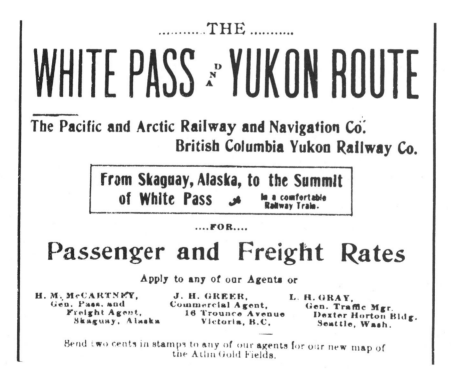

Advertising the changing times: what had been an arduous trip over the passes by foot could now be made in the comfort of a railroad car. YA

38

Units of the United States torpedo fleet tied up at the White Pass dock in Skagway in 1901.   UW

Moore's Wharf and the railroad tracks after the fire of December 14, 1914, in Skagway.   PABC

The administration building for the White Pass and Yukon Route in Skagway in 1900. It was built in 1900 and donated to the National Park Service by the Railroad in 1969.   *YA*

A loaded freight train headed for the Yukon waits to leave Skagway.   *YA*

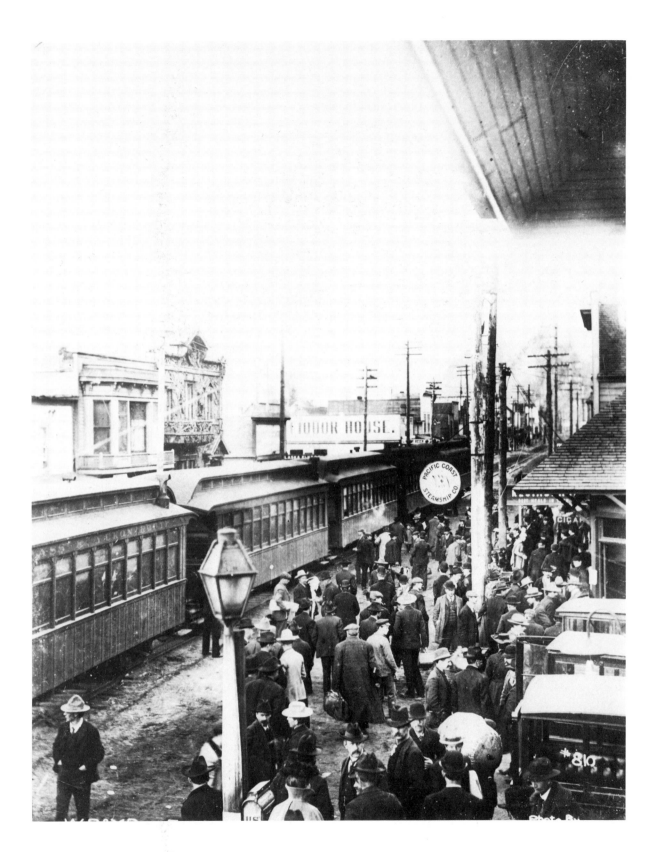

A White Pass train arriving at Skagway in the early 1900s.   *YA*

41

Skagway in the 1920s.

DP

Workshop and roundhouse at Skagway in 1899. YA

Coal bunkers at the northern end of Skagway in April 1901. YA

A White Pass excursion train crosses the small timber trestle at Rocky Point in May 1900. *YA*

A White Pass train rounds a bend on Tunnel Mountain and heads for a timber trestle in June 1901. YA

Passengers view the scenery from Porcupine Hill in the early 1900s. The railroad has been in the tourist business from the early 1900s to the present.   *UW*

The switchback near the White Pass summit in May 1899. This was used until the steel bridge was completed in 1901.   *YA*

The steel arch bridge spanning Dead Horse Gulch. The bridge was built in 1901 and was the highest steel cantilever bridge in the world when built. A roundhouse sits on the wooden trestle. Before the bridge was completed a switchback was used to negotiate the deep gorge. Trains went up the gorge and then had to back uphill to reach the summit.

YA

STEEL ARCH BRIDGE
JUNE 10, 1901

A trestle after some of its support beams collapsed. The railroad was subject to accidents like this because of the nature of the terrain. *YA*

The train station at White Pass summit, 20.4 miles from Skagway in June 1900. YA

Members of a YMCA excursion stand in flatcars at the White Pass summit in August 1899.   *YA*

Dignitaries raising flags at White Pass summit in 1914.　　　　　　*UW*

The train station at Log Cabin, British Columbia. A small town grew here during the Gold Rush and the Canadian customs collector was stationed here. The area was abandoned after the Gold Rush.　　*YA*

A freight train crosses a wooden bridge on Lewis Lake in the Yukon. The railroad has since been relocated to the east of the lake. *PABC*

Men and machine take water. Along the tracks are stacks of wood cut and piled when right-of-way was cleared. *YA*

Whitehorse on the Yukon River in 1900 was a bustling riverport and railroad terminus for the Klondike gold fields over 500 miles downriver. *YA*

Waterfront view of Whitehorse in 1920. The sternwheelers **Casca** and **Whitehorse** are docked in front of the train station. *YA*

Exterior of the Whitehorse depot, facing the waterfront in 1901. The station was built in 1900 and is still in use. *YA*

Front Street in Whitehorse at midnight June 9, 1902. *PABC*

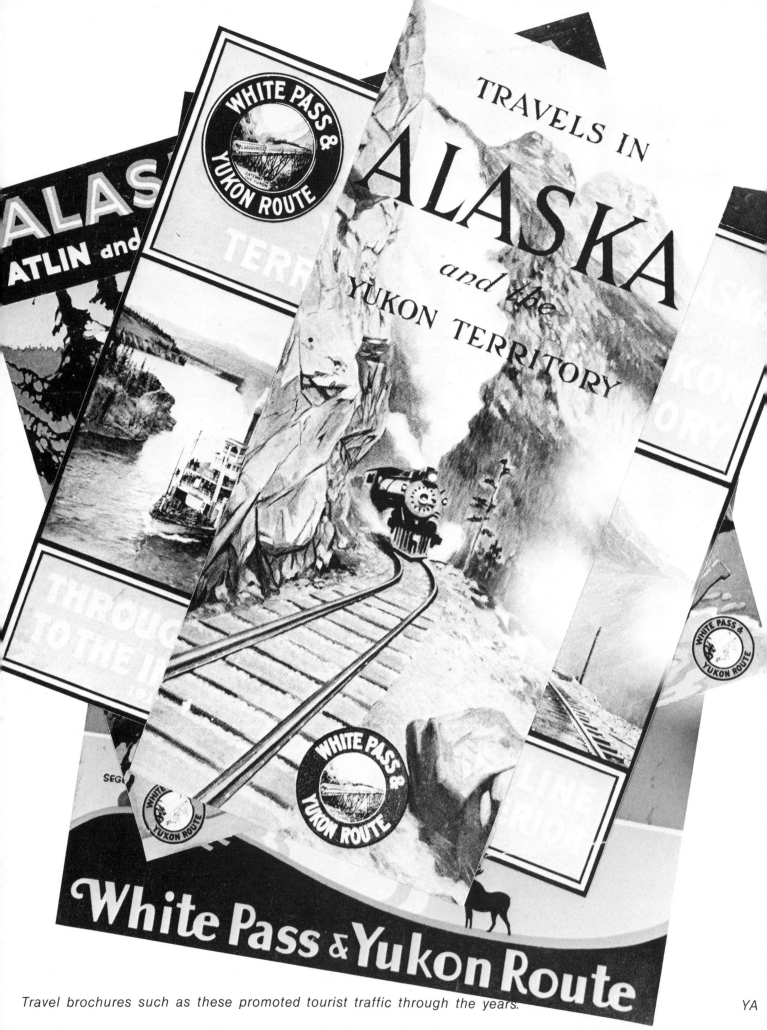

Travel brochures such as these promoted tourist traffic through the years.

OTHER OPERATIONS

The White Pass Route is much more than a railroad.

When passengers got off the train at Whitehorse in 1900, they boarded river steamers for the 460-mile trip down the Yukon to Dawson City. The service was bad, thanks to poorly constructed boats and cutthroat competition. People and freight alike were handled poorly, and in 1901 the railroad decided to start its own service. The British Yukon Navigation Company was formed to operate boats along the Yukon and offer a complete trip from Skagway to Dawson City on White Pass facilities.

Before the railroad was completed, large Yukon River steamers were built outside and brought up the Yukon, a distance of more than 4,000 miles. These boats were usually Mississippi River types and not completely suited to the Yukon. The Yukon is hard to navigate. Parts of it are narrow and sharply bending. Other parts are shallow. The current in some stretches flows at more than five miles an hour. After the railroad was built, heavy equipment could be hauled to Whitehorse, and boats suited to the river could be constructed there. The river service was extended to the inland lakes of the Yukon and northern British Columbia. Up to 100 passengers and 300 tons of freight could be carried on a typical river steamer with a four-foot draught. Their speed was 15 miles an hour. The cargo was carried on the bottom deck just above water line, along with the engines and boilers. All was enclosed by a freight house. On top of this was the passenger deck and above this the crew deck. The pilot house was on top, more than 30 feet above water level. The boats were powered by steam produced at first by wood and later by oil. They could push loaded barges in front of them. The trip downstream from Whitehorse to Dawson averaged three days and the trip upstream between five and six days. A round trip from Skagway to Dawson and return by train and steamer cost $100 in 1908.

Service was provided by these boats until September 1, 1955, when competition from highways and airplanes persuaded the company to discontinue its river business. The company actually wanted to end the river division in the early 1950s, but waited until the Klondike Highway was completed. The remains of the more than 250 boats that worked the river and lakes can still be seen along the river from Atlin to Dawson City.

In addition to steamers, which ran only in the summer, the company operated the Yukon Stage Line between Whitehorse and Dawson City from 1901 to 1921, using wagons in summer and sleighs in winter. The company also took over Canadian and United States mail contracts in 1900. The U. S. contract linked Juneau, White Pass, to St. Michael and Nome, while the Canadian contract tied Skagway to Dawson and

Atlin.

The winter contract required that dog teams be used, but the railroad was not interested in getting into the dog business and took the winter contract only to get the mail business for the full year. It sublet the American contract from Dawson west, and in the summer of 1901, after arranging to replace the dogs with horses, it took all its dogs to an island in Lake LaBarge near Whitehorse and sold them.

The Yukon Stage Line's summer wagon route opened as soon as the ice and snow left the trail and stayed in operation until late fall.

On November 2, 1902, the first horse-drawn sleigh left Whitehorse for Dawson, inaugurating horse-drawn mail freight and passenger service. The early sleighs traveled on the frozen river, but in 1903, the "Overland Trail" was constructed and the distance was shortened to 350 miles. Depending on weather conditions, a typical trip could take five to six days with relay stables and rest stops every 20 to 25 miles. The trail was very difficult at times with drifted snow, high winds and low temperatures. In the summer the steamers could haul the hay and oats by river for winter use along the trail.

Each sleigh drawn by four to six horses, could hold 9 to 14 people and carry 1,000 pounds of passenger baggage and 1,000 pounds of mail and express. In 1906 a one-way trip from Whitehorse to Dawson cost $125 by wagon and $80 to $100 by sleigh.

After 1921, other contractors took over the winter trail, and trucks and tractors were used to haul the sleighs. In 1937 the airplane took over all winter freight hauling and kept it until the new Klondike Highway was completed in 1955.

In 1916 the company opened the Atlin Inn on Lake Atlin and operated it for years along with motor launches on the lake.

In the 1920s and 30s, the airplane was coming into its own and air routes were established throughout northern Canada and Alaska. The company got into the airline business in 1934, flying a regular route among Whitehorse, Dawson and Mayo. In 1936, Ford Tri-motors, the most modern plane of the period, were purchased. They could carry 12 passengers. In December 1941, Yukon Southern Air Transport bought out the business, just before the railroad was called on to join in the war effort.

A bus line, the British Yukon Navigation Company, was established by the railroad along the Alaska Highway after the war. It also built hotels and rest stops along the highway and operated refrigerator trucks between Dawson Creek and Whitehorse for many years.

Opening the Klondike Highway in 1955 spelled the doom for the river boats, but opened up the Yukon interior to truck traffic and consequently to heavy mineral exploration. Large quantities of asbestos ore were discovered at Cassier in northern British Columbia and just northwest of Dawson City, and trucks were used to haul the product to Whitehorse for shipment to Skagway and Vancouver. This business ended in the 1970s. Mineral concentrates are still hauled to Whitehorse by White Pass trucks over an extensive road system today.

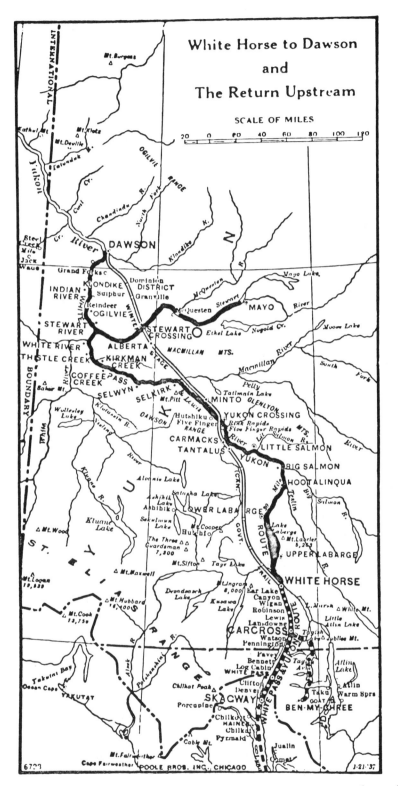

The route of the railroad, winter stage line and summer steamers from Skagway to Dawson.

YA

MAP 3

The sternwheeler **Casca** *ready to sail from Dawson to Whitehorse on October 11, 1908.* *SC*

The sternwheeler **Klondike** *on display at Whitehorse. The original* **Klondike** *was built in the early 1900s but sank. The present one was built in 1937, using part of the machinery of the original boat. She is 210 feet long and 44 feet wide and was used for many years to haul ore from Mayo to Whitehorse. It was modified several times to accommodate passengers but was finally withdrawn from service in 1955. The railroad donated the boat to the Canadian Government for preservation as a historic site.* *SC*

The sternwheelers **Tutshi** and **Gleaner** docked at Carcross in 1920. The **Tutshi** was a tourist steamer that operated from Carcross to Ben-my-Chree on the south end of Tagish Lake for many years.   YA

The **Tutshi** on permanent display at Carcross.   SC

The Sternwheeler **Keno** docked at Dawson City. It was built in 1922 and brought to Dawson in 1960 for permanent display by Parks Canada.   SC

Sternwheelers resting in dry dock at Whitehorse in 1944 with the railroad tracks in the foreground.
                                                                          USA

A Royal Mail wagon on display at Carcross. *SC*

Winter travel on the White Pass Stage Line which operated from 1901 to 1921 between Whitehorse and Dawson. *YA*

The railroad's first airplane - an amphibious plane nicknamed **"the Duck"**---*beached along the Yukon River at Dawson in 1935.*　　　　　　　　　　　　*YA*

A Curtis Condor owned by the railroad. It flew regularly between Dawson, Whitehorse and Mayo from 1937 to 1940.　　　　　　　　　　　　*YA*

SNOW

Most railroads in Canada and the northern United States, and in mountainous regions elsewhere in the continent, have to contend with snow. The White Pass Route, however, faces a unique snow problem as it crosses the Coastal Range, a region of tremendous snowfalls and extra-ordinarily rugged terrain. The snow is still a problem today, although modern equipment has made it less a menace than it was during the con-struction period 80 years ago.

Snowfall is especially heavy on the grade to White Pass and Log Cabin. Temperatures here can reach 60 degrees or more below zero.

A snowfall of many feet is not uncommon, and immense snowslides and drifts occur every winter. A rail-road needs exceptional snow-removal equipment to operate in these condi-tions.

The White Pass Route bought Cooke rotary snowplows, built before 1898, to keep the rails clear. In the early days, even these big plows could not always get through, and passengers and crew sometimes had to dig the train out by hand. Ice on the tracks was another problem. It had to be watched and removed constantly.

The first winter of construction, 1898-99, was one of the worst in history, but building continued.

During the second winter, 1899-1900, snow began falling December 17 and continued for a month. Between Skagway and Bennett drifts were 8 to 12 feet deep. Temperatures ranged from 30 to 60 degrees below zero and the wind blew constantly. From March 7 to 11, a great storm raged. A rotary plow and train left Skagway March 7 and did not reach Bennett, 40 miles away, until four days later. Snowslides brought down boulders that had to be pulled off the tracks with chains. There was constant danger that the rotary plows, pushed by steam engines, would hit large boulders or a loose rail.

The roadbed had to be solid to handle the rotary plows. These had big boilers and powerful engines. A set of large blades or knives was housed in a wheel on the front of each plow. The blades revolved and sliced the snow as the plow was pushed forward by a locomotive. Snow was pushed out and to the side of the tracks by centrifugal force. Snow deeper than twelve feet had to be cut by hand before the plows could slice through the drifts. The maximum speed a plow could attain was one to five miles an hour.

The troops who took over the railroad during World War II faced some of the worst winters since the construction days of 1898-1900. Even with the help of bulldozers the rotary snowplows couldn't keep up, and the line closed for 10 days in 1943 and 18 days in 1944. The temperature dropped so low that the engine wheels froze to the rails. Some of the rolling stock that had been sent north to help in the war traffic just was not suited to the extreme temperatures.

One train was stranded at Fraser Loop for seven days by snowslides and drifts. A tractor crossed frozen Lake Bennett from Carcross to rescue the crew, which had burned the furniture to keep from freezing.

The old rotary plows were retired in the 1950s, and specially equipped bulldozers stationed along the tracks now keep the rails clear. Snow remains a continuous winter problem, however, particularly up to the White Pass summit.

CLEARING THE TRACK AFTER A SNOW STORM ON THE SUMMIT OF WHITE PASS AND YUKON ROUTE, MAR. 20-99

Workmen clear the tracks after a blizzard on the summit of the White Pass Route in March 1899.   *UW*

Three White Pass employees standing in front of a rotary snowplow on the tracks near the tunnel in December 1899.   *YA*

A rotary clears the rails in the early 1900s.   *PABC*

Crew members ham it up as engine No. 7 pauses between snowbanks near Glacier in December 1899. *YA*

Snowbound at the summit in 1915. *YA*

*A rotary snowplow drives 16-foot drifts ahead of it during the winter of
1942-43.*   *USA*

A rotary plow digs through a snowbank during the winter of 1943-44.   *USA*

The rotaries were retired in the 1950s, and these especially adapted bulldozers are now used to remove snow along the right-of-way. DP

Supplies vital to the Yukon are shipped year-round on the White Pass Route. WP & YR

WAR YEARS

The United States' entry into World War II and the decision to build the Alaska (Alcan) Highway had a profound effect on the White Pass Route. The highway was to be built from Dawson Creek, British Columbia, to Fairbanks, Alaska, through the northern part of British Columbia, the southern Yukon and the interior of Alaska.

It was to be a rush project designed to meet a real threat to Alaska by Japanese forces in the early days of the war. The inland route was selected because it was out of range of Japanese air and naval forces and crossed less-rugged mountains than those of the coast. This route also would connect a string of air bases stretching from Edmonton, Alberta, to Fairbanks, Alaska.

The road was to be built by American troops with American money through mostly Canadian territory in order to permit overland shipment of war material to Alaska and northern Canada.

The 1,500-mile route provided only three main access points for the thousands of men and tons of material building up in the south.

One was Dawson Creek, British Columbia, at the southern terminus of the road. Dawson Creek was the end of the Northern Alberta Railroad and was connected by road to Edmonton, Alberta, and points south. The second was Fairbanks, the northern terminus of the highway. Fairbanks was connected to Anchorage and the sea by the Alaska Railroad and the Richardson Highway.

The third was Whitehorse, the terminus of the most important link to the interior of the Yukon: the White Pass Route from Skagway. Men and materials could be shipped up the inside passage to Skagway, hauled on the railroad to Whitehorse, and then sent north and south along the highway.

In addition to supplying the Alaska Highway project in 1942-43, the railroad carried material for the CANOL construction project, a road and pipeline built by the U. S. Army from Norman Wells, Northwest Territories, to pipe oil to a Whitehorse refinery used by the military.

Construction of the highway began in March 1942, and it was determined at once that help was needed to keep the trains running.

Although the railroad could handle peacetime demand, it was overwhelmed by the quantity of material needed for the two construction projects. The docks at Skagway and the railroad's equipment were both inadequate. Most of the equipment, left over from the Gold Rush days, was practically worn out. Fewer than a dozen engines were in working order and the roadbed was desperately in need of repair.

So the railroad was leased to the U. S. government for the duration of the war, and the U. S. Army took over its operation, retaining the civilian employees. The 770th Railway Operating Battalion of the Military Railway Service officially assumed control on October 1, 1942, and operated the White Pass Route until the war was over. Most of the men in the battalion were from Southern states, and on their official introduction to the north country, they encountered one of the worst winters in its history. Construction was started on many buildings and shops in Skagway and Whitehorse to accommodate the troops and material being assembled for construction of the road.

Rolling stock was built at the repair yards in Skagway and even one of the old locomotives that had run to the Klondike gold fields was pressed into service.

Engines Nos. 10 and 14 were shipped north in 1942 by the Army. They had been built originally for the East Tennessee and Western North Carolina Railroad. Engines Nos. 20 and 21 came from the Colorado and Southern Railroad, and Engines Nos. 22, 23 and 24 from the Silverton Northern, in 1943. All of these locomotives had been built by Baldwin in the late 1890s and early 1900s.

In 1943, ten steam engines consigned to Iran were diverted to Skagway, converted from metered gauge to the three-foot gauge and used for the rest of the war. The engines, all 2-8-2s (a wheel alignment designation) built by Baldwin for the U. S. Army, were numbered 190 through 200. All were scrapped or sold after the war except No. 195, which is on display at the Trail of 98 Museum in Skagway.

Seven additional narrow-gauge engines built in 1923 by American Locomotive were purchased from the Denver, Rio Grande and Western Railroad in 1942 and used until 1945.

During the war the railroad accumulated 36 engines and almost 300 freight cars, some built for service in South America. More than 280,000 tons of material were carried to Whitehorse in 1943---45,000 tons in August alone. Thousands of troops and construction workers were also carried in both directions.

At the height of operations in 1943, dozens of trains rolled between Skagway and Whitehorse every day. As the war approached its end, the pressure eased, and none too soon. The railroad was literally worn out.

The 770th Railway Operating Battalion continued to run the railroad until control was returned to the pre-war management on May 1, 1946.

The Skagway dock in September 1942. The docks were totally inadequate for the tons of construction materials that were flowing into the port from the south. USA

Skagway in April 1945, was not the bustling port of 1942, but still was an important point for the trans-shipment of war material by rail to the Yukon and interior Alaska. USA

Vehicles headed north for the Alaska Highway through Skagway in 1942.   AA

Troops boarding the train at Skagway for Whitehorse. Some of the passenger cars were left over from the Gold Rush days 42 years earlier.   USA

The only crossing of the railroad and the Alaska Highway was located just east of Whitehorse in 1944. USA

Troops of Company B, 770th Railway Battalion, at Skagway in March 1944. They had taken over operation of the railroad in October 1942, for the duration of the war, and proved to be efficient railroad managers. DP

Main Street in Whitehorse, 1944.   *USA*

Warehouses and construction materials by the White Pass tracks on the outskirts of Whitehorse in 1944. From here supplies could be tucked up and down the newly completed Alaska Highway.   *USA*

MODERN DAY OPERATIONS

The White Pass Route today is an integral part of Federal Industries, Ltd., a Canadian-owned diveresified transportation company. The White Pass and Yukon Corporation, Ltd., is composed of the railroad, container ship, highway truck transport and petroleum divisions. They serve the Yukon, *northern* British Columbia, Alberta, Northwest Territories and Alaska.

The railroad is primarily a freight-hauling line, carrying bulk mineral ore concentrates from interior Yukon to Skagway, and returning general freight and petroleum products into the interior. It also carries more than 70,000 tourists a year, either on a round-trip from Skagway to Lake Bennett or from Skagway through to Whitehorse. The railroad has more than 400 units of rolling stock. The corporation employs 1,000 people in all divisions.

Ore concentrates from the Yukon mines account for the largest share of today's business. More than 500,000 tons of lead, zinc and copper concentrates are trucked annually from mines at Faro-Anvil and the Mayo-Elsa-Keno districts on specially designed White Pass trucks and teardrop containers to Whitehorse, then loaded on railroad cars for the haul to Skagway. The concentrates are unloaded at the Bulk Storage and Loading Terminal, which has a capacity of 100,000 tons. The concentrates are shipped to Vancouver and points overseas on ocean freighters capable of carrying 30,000 to 35,000 tons each.

The White Pass Route pioneered the construction of container ships, building the world's first such vessel, the **Clifford J. Rogers**, in 1955. The **Clifford J. Rogers** was retired in 1965, but two successor container ships, the 6,500-ton **Frank H. Brown** and her sister ship, the **Klondike**, ply the waters between Skagway and Vancouver for White Pass.

The White Pass truck line is the major carrier of the bulk ore concentrates, but also hauls general freight and heavy equipment. A wholly owned subsidiary---Loiselle Transport---operates out of Edmonton, Alberta, and serves northwestern Canada with general freight and equipment hauling.

Petroleum products are delivered by train and pipeline from Skagway to Whitehorse and then moved by truck to various points in the Yukon and northern British Columbia. The company also handles auto trade products.

The White Pass and Yukon Corporation is an innovative leader in its field.

Modern Skagway. It has a population of 700 and is a major tourist area of Alaska. *NPS*

Broadway Street in Skagway. Much of the flavor of the Gold Rush still lingers, and part of the town has been included in the Klondike National Historical Park. *NPS*

The ore loading docks at Skagway.   DP

The White Pass passenger terminal in Skagway.   It was completed in 1969.   SC

The railroad shop in Skagway. It was built in 1969 to replace the original roundhouse and shops, which burned down.   *SC*

Old engine sheds at the Skagway shops.   *SC*

One of the original buildings put up by the U. S. Army in 1942 for the Skagway
shops.   *SC*

The roadbed cut into the rock on the way to the summit. The new Skagway-Carcross
Highway is on the mountainside at the right.   *SC*

Dead Horse Gulch as seen from the railroad. Thousands of horses died here in 1897-98, driven to their death by the gold-crazed prospectors. *SC*

A sign marks the trail of the stampeders of 1897-98 below the White Pass summit. *SC*

The steel cantilever bridge as it appears today. It was abandoned in 1969 when the new shorter bridge and tunnel were completed.   *SC*

The new bridge and tunnel below the summit, completed in 1969. It replaced the steel cantilever bridge built in 1901.   *DP*

Buildings on the Alaska-British Columbia border at the White Pass summit.   *SC*

Remains of a U. S. Army pumping station just north of the White Pass summit. Such stations were built along the right-of-way during World War II to pump oil from Skagway to Whitehorse for the construction of the Alaska Highway.   *SC*

The Carcross Station, built in 1902 and enlarged in 1925. The golden spike ceremony marking the completion of the railroad was held here on July 29, 1900.   *SC*

The last original building on the railroad at Fraser faces the new Canadian customs building across the Carcross-Skagway road. The old building was a water tank for locomotives and rotary snowplows. A turn-a-round was provided there for the equipment.   *SC*

The White Pass and Yukon Route station at the north end of Main Street in Whitehorse. It was built in 1899 and remodeled in 1953. SC

Waterfront view of Whitehorse, Yukon. SC

*The **Clifford J. Rogers** at Skagway. It was built in 1955 as the world's first ship designed especially for container cargo. It was retired in 1965.* DP

*The **Frank H. Brown** at Skagway. It was built along with the **Klondike** in 1965 to carry container cargo between Skagway and Vancouver, British Columbia.* DP

Trains meeting at Lake Bennett in the 1960's.   WP & YR

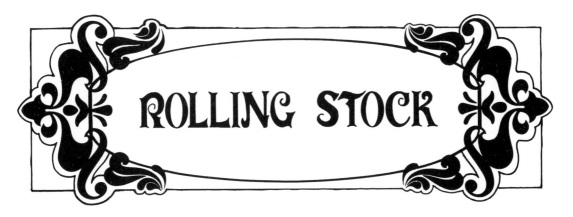

ROLLING STOCK

In its 80 years, the White Pass and Yukon Route has acquired many types of locomotives and a colorful assortment of freight and passenger cars. The last of 53 steam locomotives was retired in 1964, but most of the two dozen gas and diesel locomotives acquired since 1942 are still in service. The railroad had about 438 units of all types in its 1978 inventory.

All the early locomotives were obtained from other railroads and converted to run on narrow-gauge tracks of the White Pass Route.

The first steam engine brought north in 1898 (and now on display at Skagway), had been used on the Utah and Northern and the Columbia and Puget Sound railroads. It bore the number 1 until 1900, when it was rebuilt and redesignated No. 52. It was retired in 1940.

Engines 3, 4 and 5 were built in the 1880s and 90s and brought north in 1899, renumbered 56 in 1900 and scrapped in 1938. Engines 59, 60, 61 and 62 were built for the railroad in 1900 and ended up as rip-rap in the Skagway River in the late 1940s.

Engines 63 through 69 were built between the 1870s and the early 1900s. They were scrapped or sold to other railroads after many years of service.

No new engines were purchased between 1908 and 1938 because of adverse economic conditions.

Engines 70 and 71, the last acquired before World War II, were bought in 1938 and 1939. No. 72 was built in 1947 and retired in 1964. Engines 80 and 81 were built in 1920 for the Sumpter Valley Railroad. They were bought by the White Pass in 1940 and were retired in the late 1950s.

The rolling stock inventory changed drastically to meet the tremendous demands of the military buildup, so engines were picked up whenever they could be found. No. 4 was bought from the defunct Klondike Mines Railway at Dawson City. No. 10 and No. 14 came from the East Tennessee and Western North Carolina Railroad. No. 20 and No. 21 were built in 1890 for the Denver, Leadville and Gunnison Railroad. Nos. 22, 23 and 24 were built in 1904 for the Silverton Northern Railroad. Eleven locomotives -- 190 through 200 -- were built in 1943 for use in Iran but were diverted to Skagway, converted there for narrow-gauge service, and used for the rest of the war. All were scrapped after the war except No. 195, which is on display at Skagway. Nos. 250 through 256 were built in 1923 for the Denver, Rio Grande and Western Railroad and brought north by the army in 1942. All were scrapped after the war.

The age of diesel locomotives came to the White Pass in 1954 with the purchase of units 90 through 100. These were 80-ton 800-horsepower type C-C, 6-cylinder diesel units built by General Electric especially designed for the White Pass Route. Nos. 101 through 107 were built by Alco in Montreal and delivered in 1969. Nos. 108 through 110 were bought in 1972 from Alco. In all the company acquired 22 diesel engines, including the second No. 81, a diesel-electric switcher built in 1957 for the U. S. Army. Nos. 102 and 108 were destroyed in 1969 when the roundhouse and shops at Skagway burned down.

Freight cars on the railroad evolved from the wooden box cars, cabooses and primitive oil tank cars of the early years to the all steel cars and ore concentrate carriers of today. The repair shops at Skagway are capable of repairing or rebuilding most of the rolling stock.

The passenger cars are a mixed breed. Some date back to the early 1900s. The new ones are of all steel construction. All bear names of prominent places in the area. Approximately 30 coaches, parlor cars, baggage cars and combination cars are in service.

The **Duchess** *on display at Carcross. It was first built as a 2'6" gauge engine and widened to the 3-foot gauge when sold to the White Pass in 1899. Retired in 1910.* *SC*

The railroad's first locomotive, brought north in 1898 after long service on the Utah and Northern Railroad. It was built in 1881, rebuilt in 1900, renumbered No. 52 and retired in 1940. DP

Locomotive No. 1 (renumbered 52) on display at Skagway. WP & YR

Engine No. 59, built in 1900, pulls four smaller locomotives on Broadway in Skagway. It was scrapped in 1941. Vancouver Public Library

Engine No. 7 leaving Skagway for the Summit in 1900. UW

Locomotives Nos. 4 and 5, along with passenger and baggage cars, stand on a Seattle dock awaiting shipment to Skagway in 1898.   PABC

Engine No. 5, built for the Columbia and Puget Sound Railroad and sold to the White Pass in 1898. It was renumbered No. 55 in 1900 and sold in 1904 to the Klondike Mines Railway. It is now on display at Dawson City.   UW

93

Engine No. 71, built for the White Pass in 1939 by the Baldwin Locomotive Works and retired in 1963. *DP*

The remains of Engine No. 71 at the Skagway shops. It was built in 1939 and retired in 1963. *PABC*

Engine No. 81 after unloading at the Skagway dock in 1940. It was built in 1920 for the Sumpter Valley Railroad and retired in 1957. *DP*

Engine No. 73 was on display at Bennett but has been moved to Whitehorse for restoration. It was built in 1947 and retired in 1964. *SC*

Klondike Mines Railway engines Nos. 1, 2 and 3 on display at Dawson City, Yukon. All were purchased from the White Pass in the early 1900s. SC

Rotary snowplow No. 1 on display at Bennett. The rotaries were replaced in the 1950s by the bulldozers used today. SC

Locomotive No. 20, loaned to the White Pass by the Colorado and Southern Railroad during World War II. This photo was taken in Seattle in 1946. PABC

Engine No. 196 at the Skagway yards during World War II. It was built in 1943 and retired in 1961. DP

Engine No. 70 was built for the White Pass in 1938 by the Baldwin Locomotive Works and retired in 1963. Here it stands on the turntable at Skagway.   *DP*

Gas-powered engine No. 3, built in 1942 and used as a yard switcher until it was scrapped in 1969.   *DP*

A row of diesel engines at the Skagway yard. They were built by Alco between 1969 and 1972 and are still in use.   SC

Diesel engine No. 93, built for the White Pass in 1956 by General Electric, stands at the Skagway station.   DP

Ore from the Keno Hill mine stands on wooden flat cars in the 1950s.   *DP*

Ore cars being unloaded at the Skagway dock.   *DP*

Lowboy flat car built
at the Skagway shops.

DP

Older style tank car.

DP

New type tank car now
used on the railroad.

DP

A steel caboose.

SC

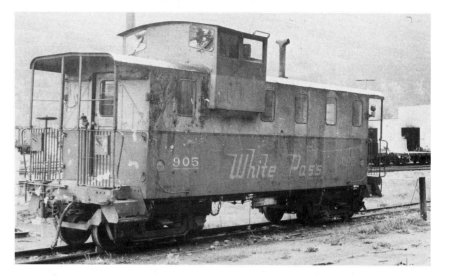

A wooden boxcar.

DP

General cargo containers on new all-steel flatcars.

DP

An older passenger car.

DP

One of the newer steel passenger cars.

DP

An older baggage car, still in use.

DP

A wooden combination baggage and passenger car.

DP

RAILROAD FACTS

Construction Began .... May 28, 1898

Reached White Pass .... February 20, 1899

Reached Lake Bennett .... July 6, 1899

End of Construction .... July 29, 1900

Length in Alaska .... 20.4 Miles

Length in British Columbia .... 30.9 Miles

Length in Yukon .... 59.1 Miles

Total Length .... 110.4 Miles

Cubic Yards of Material Moved (1898-1900) 1,431,600

Cubic Yards of Snow Shoveled (1898-1900) 476,000

Average Grade to Summit Per Mile .... 141 Feet

Maximum Grade to Summit Per Mile .... 206 Feet

Highest Elevation .... 2,940 Feet

White Pass Summit Elevation .... 2,865 Feet

Gauge .... 3 Feet

Maximum Curvature - 16 Degree Radius .... 359.3 Feet

Tunnel Length (1900) .... 245 Feet

Snow Sheds Length (1900) .... 3,157 Feet

Cost of Construction .... $10 Million